Prepare for Medicare

THE INSIDER'S GUIDE™ USERNAME AND PASSWORD BOOK

Internet Username, Login, Password, Website and Journal Logbook with Tabs

Never Lose a Login or Password Again!
Categories Tabbed for Easy Reference and Include:
Email, Cellphone, Banking, Shopping, Memberships, Streaming Services, Travel, Security, WiFi and Much More!

Matt Feret

If found, please call/text:

....

Cash award:

$ ....

Matt Feret is an author, the host of The Matt Feret Show and a twenty-year veteran of the Medicare insurance industry. Matt is passionate about helping people prepare, organize and navigate a path towards a successful retirement.

www.PrepareforMedicare.com

www.PrepareforSocialSecurity.com

www.PrepareforPassing.com

www.TheMattFeretShow.com

Paperback ISBN: 978-1-7372122-0-3

Hardcover ISBN: 978-1-7372122-7-0

Disclaimer: For personal use only. The publisher is not responsible or liable for loss or damage that may occur as a result of storing information in this publication. This publication should not be considered secure password storage device and should be stored in a secure location when not in use. This publication is in no way sponsored, associated, authorized, approved, endorsed nor, in any way affiliated with any company, trademarked names, or other marks. Any such mention is for purpose of reference only. Please keep this in a secure location as it will contain private and personal information when completed.

★ ★ ★ ★ ★

PROUDLY DESIGNED AND MADE IN THE USA

PASSWORD BASICS

Picking a good password is the most important thing you can do to preserve the privacy of your personal data, online accounts and information. A secure password should be:

- ✓ **Known only to you**
- ✓ **Long enough to be secure (more than 12 characters)**
- ✓ **Hard to guess – even by a family member**
- ✓ **Easy for you to recall**
- ✓ **Easy for you to type accurately**
- ✓ **A combination of letters, numbers and symbols**

Disable auto form-filling on your web browsers. Automatically filling forms in the browser has made breaking into accounts easier. Don't answer "yes" when browsers ask you to save passwords. Websites and companies have and will continue to be hacked.

IT'S IMPORTANT TO NEVER RE-USE PASSWORDS.

Certain companies like Apple, Meta (Facebook and Instagram) and Google allow users to bequeath account access to a designee. This person would be allowed to download your data and access your profiles after your passing, but not necessarily your passwords. You may be able to limit what the legacy contact can access after you pass.

Some companies also allow users to create a "memorialized" account. You must identify this person prior to your passing, and communicate your wishes to the company as well as the legacy contact. Not every company features these options and if they do, are most often found under your account settings.

MY INFORMATION

Full Name: ....

Maiden Name: ....

Other Names Used: ....

DOB: ....

Home Phone Number: ....

Cell Phone Number: ....

Work Phone Number: ....

Personal Email: ....

Password/Hint: ....

Password/Hint: ....

Work/School Email: ....

Password/Hint: ....

Password/Hint: ....

Additional Email: ....

Password/Hint: ....

Password/Hint: ....

Current Home Address: ....

....

....

Other Addresses: ....

....

....

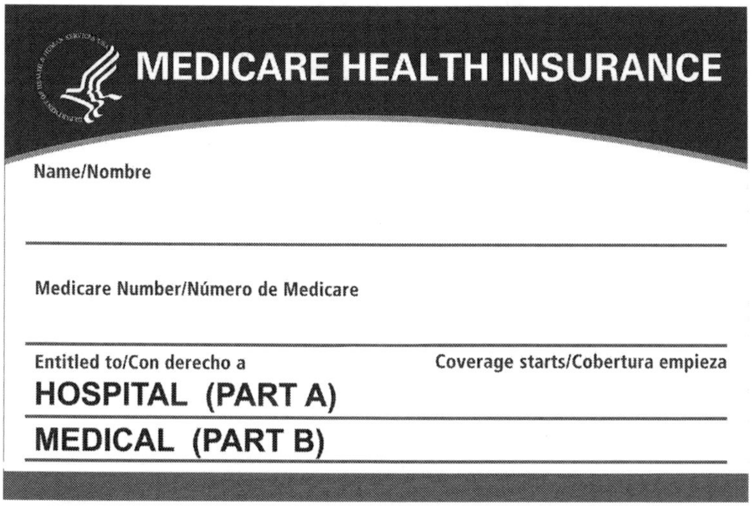
MEDICARE HEALTH INSURANCE
Name/Nombre
Medicare Number/Número de Medicare
Entitled to/Con derecho a
Coverage starts/Cobertura empieza
HOSPITAL (PART A)
MEDICAL (PART B)

SOCIAL SECURITY
SOCIAL SECURITY ADMINISTRATION
THIS NUMBER HAS BEEN ESTABLISHED FOR
SIGNATURE

MEDICARE.GOV

Website Address: www.medicare.gov

Username:

Password/Hint:

Code/PIN:

Phone:

Notes:

mySOCIALSECURITY

Website Address: www.ssa.gov

Username:

Password/Hint:

Code/PIN:

Phone:

Notes:

LOGIN.GOV

Website Address: www.login.gov

Username: ....

Password/Hint: ....

....

....

Code/PIN: ....

Phone: ....

Notes: ....

....

MY MEDICARE INSURANCE

Aetna, Humana, United Healthcare, etc.

App/Website/Company Name: ....

Website Address: ....

Username: ....

Password/Hint: ....

....

....

Code/PIN: ....

Phone: ....

Notes: ....

....

MY MEDICARE INSURANCE

Aetna, Humana, United Healthcare, etc.

App/Website/Company Name: ....

Website Address: ....

Username: ....

Password/Hint: ....

....

....

Code/PIN: ....

Phone: ....

Notes: ....

....

MY MEDICARE INSURANCE

Aetna, Humana, United Healthcare, etc.

App/Website/Company Name: ....

Website Address: ....

Username: ....

Password/Hint: ....

....

....

Code/PIN: ....

Phone: ....

Notes: ....

....

TABLE OF CONTENTS

IN CASE OF EMERGENCY (ICE)

Name: ....

Phone: ....

Email: ....

Relation: ....

IMPORTANT PHONE NUMBERS

FREQUENTLY USED (DAILY/WEEKLY)

Cell Phone Number: ....

Phone PIN: ....

App/Website/Company Account Username: ....

Password/Hint: ....

Notes: ....

TABLET OR IPAD

Account Username: ....

Password/Hint: ....

....

Code/PIN: ....

Notes: ....

....

....

....

....

PERSONAL COMPUTER

Account Username: ....

Password/Hint: ....

....

Code/PIN: ....

Notes ....

....

....

....

....

WORK COMPUTER

Account Username: ....

Password/Hint: ....

....

Code/PIN: ....

Notes ....

....

....

....

....

SCHOOL COMPUTER

Account Username: ....

Password/Hint: ....

....

Code/PIN: ....

Notes ....

....

....

....

....

CLOUD STORAGE

Dropbox, iCloud, OneDrive, etc.

App/Website/Company Name: ....

Website Address: ....

Username: ....

Password/Hint: ....

....

....

Code/PIN: ....

Phone: ....

Notes: ....

....

App/Website/Company Name: ....

Website Address: ....

Username: ....

Password/Hint: ....

....

....

Code/PIN: ....

Phone: ....

Notes: ....

....

App/Website/Company Name: ....

Website Address: ....

Username: ....

Password/Hint: ....

....

....

Code/PIN: ....

Phone: ....

Notes: ....

....

App/Website/Company Name: ....

Website Address: ....

Username: ....

Password/Hint: ....

....

....

Code/PIN: ....

Phone: ....

Notes: ....

....

CLOUD STORAGE

Dropbox, iCloud, OneDrive, etc.

App/Website/Company Name: ....

Website Address: ....

Username: ....

Password/Hint: ....

....

....

Code/PIN: ....

Phone: ....

Notes: ....

....

App/Website/Company Name: ....

Website Address: ....

Username: ....

Password/Hint: ....

....

....

Code/PIN: ....

Phone: ....

Notes: ....

....

App/Website/Company Name: ....

Website Address: ....

Username: ....

Password/Hint: ....

....

....

Code/PIN: ....

Phone: ....

Notes: ....

....

App/Website/Company Name: ....

Website Address: ....

Username: ....

Password/Hint: ....

....

....

Code/PIN: ....

Phone: ....

Notes: ....

....

DATING

eharmony, Match, OkCupid, etc.

App/Website/Company Name: ....

Website Address: ....

Username: ....

Password/Hint: ....

....

....

Code/PIN: ....

Phone: ....

Notes: ....

....

App/Website/Company Name: ....

Website Address: ....

Username: ....

Password/Hint: ....

....

....

Code/PIN: ....

Phone: ....

Notes: ....

....

App/Website/Company Name: ....

Website Address: ....

Username: ....

Password/Hint: ....

....

....

Code/PIN: ....

Phone: ....

Notes: ....

....

App/Website/Company Name: ....

Website Address: ....

Username: ....

Password/Hint: ....

....

....

Code/PIN: ....

Phone: ....

Notes: ....

....

EBOOK OR AUDIOBOOK

Amazon, Apple Books, OverDrive, etc

App/Website/Company Name: ....

Website Address: ....

Username: ....

Password/Hint: ....

....

....

Code/PIN: ....

Phone: ....

Notes: ....

....

App/Website/Company Name: ....

Website Address: ....

Username: ....

Password/Hint: ....

....

....

Code/PIN: ....

Phone: ....

Notes: ....

....

App/Website/Company Name: ....

Website Address: ....

Username: ....

Password/Hint: ....

....

....

Code/PIN: ....

Phone: ....

Notes: ....

....

App/Website/Company Name: ....

Website Address: ....

Username: ....

Password/Hint: ....

....

....

Code/PIN: ....

Phone: ....

Notes: ....

....

FITNESS

Fitbit, Garmin, Apple Watch, etc.

App/Website/Company Name:

Website Address:

Username:

Password/Hint:

Code/PIN:

Phone:

Notes:

App/Website/Company Name:

Website Address:

Username:

Password/Hint:

Code/PIN:

Phone:

Notes:

App/Website/Company Name:

Website Address:

Username:

Password/Hint:

Code/PIN:

Phone:

Notes:

App/Website/Company Name:

Website Address:

Username:

Password/Hint:

Code/PIN:

Phone:

Notes:

FOOD

Dominos, Grubhub, Uber Eats, etc.

App/Website/Company Name: ....

Website Address: ....

Username: ....

Password/Hint: ....

....

....

Code/PIN: ....

Phone: ....

Notes: ....

....

App/Website/Company Name: ....

Website Address: ....

Username: ....

Password/Hint: ....

....

....

Code/PIN: ....

Phone: ....

Notes: ....

....

App/Website/Company Name: ....

Website Address: ....

Username: ....

Password/Hint: ....

....

....

Code/PIN: ....

Phone: ....

Notes: ....

....

App/Website/Company Name: ....

Website Address: ....

Username: ....

Password/Hint: ....

....

....

Code/PIN: ....

Phone: ....

Notes: ....

....

FOOD

Dominos, Grubhub, Uber Eats, etc.

App/Website/Company Name: ....

Website Address: ....

Username: ....

Password/Hint: ....

....

....

Code/PIN: ....

Phone: ....

Notes: ....

....

App/Website/Company Name: ....

Website Address: ....

Username: ....

Password/Hint: ....

....

....

Code/PIN: ....

Phone: ....

Notes: ....

....

App/Website/Company Name: ....

Website Address: ....

Username: ....

Password/Hint: ....

....

....

Code/PIN: ....

Phone: ....

Notes: ....

....

App/Website/Company Name: ....

Website Address: ....

Username: ....

Password/Hint: ....

....

....

Code/PIN: ....

Phone: ....

Notes: ....

....

APPS AND WEBSITES

FINANCE

HOME AND SECURITY

NETWORK

OTHER

FOOD

Dominos, Grubhub, Uber Eats, etc.

App/Website/Company Name: ....

Website Address: ....

Username: ....

Password/Hint: ....

....

....

Code/PIN: ....

Phone: ....

Notes: ....

....

App/Website/Company Name: ....

Website Address: ....

Username: ....

Password/Hint: ....

....

....

Code/PIN: ....

Phone: ....

Notes: ....

....

App/Website/Company Name: ....

Website Address: ....

Username: ....

Password/Hint: ....

....

....

Code/PIN: ....

Phone: ....

Notes: ....

....

App/Website/Company Name: ....

Website Address: ....

Username: ....

Password/Hint: ....

....

....

Code/PIN: ....

Phone: ....

Notes: ....

....

APPS AND WEBSITES
FINANCE
HOME AND SECURITY
NETWORK
OTHER

GAMES

Chess, Empires and Puzzles, Wordle, etc.

App/Website/Company Name: ....

Website Address: ....

Username: ....

Password/Hint: ....

....

....

Code/PIN: ....

Phone: ....

Notes: ....

....

App/Website/Company Name: ....

Website Address: ....

Username: ....

Password/Hint: ....

....

....

Code/PIN: ....

Phone: ....

Notes: ....

....

App/Website/Company Name: ....

Website Address: ....

Username: ....

Password/Hint: ....

....

....

Code/PIN: ....

Phone: ....

Notes: ....

....

App/Website/Company Name: ....

Website Address: ....

Username: ....

Password/Hint: ....

....

....

Code/PIN: ....

Phone: ....

Notes: ....

....

GAMES

Chess, Empires and Puzzles, Wordle, etc.

App/Website/Company Name: ....

Website Address: ....

Username: ....

Password/Hint: ....

....

....

Code/PIN: ....

Phone: ....

Notes: ....

....

App/Website/Company Name: ....

Website Address: ....

Username: ....

Password/Hint: ....

....

....

Code/PIN: ....

Phone: ....

Notes: ....

....

APPS AND WEBSITES
FINANCE
HOME AND SECURITY
NETWORK
OTHER

App/Website/Company Name: ....

Website Address: ....

Username: ....

Password/Hint: ....

....

....

Code/PIN: ....

Phone: ....

Notes: ....

....

App/Website/Company Name: ....

Website Address: ....

Username: ....

Password/Hint: ....

....

....

Code/PIN: ....

Phone: ....

Notes: ....

....

HEALTH

Calm, MyFitnessPal, Teladoc, etc.

App/Website/Company Name: ....

Website Address: ....

Username: ....

Password/Hint: ....

....

....

Code/PIN: ....

Phone: ....

Notes: ....

....

App/Website/Company Name: ....

Website Address: ....

Username: ....

Password/Hint: ....

....

....

Code/PIN: ....

Phone: ....

Notes: ....

....

App/Website/Company Name: ....

Website Address: ....

Username: ....

Password/Hint: ....

....

....

Code/PIN: ....

Phone: ....

Notes: ....

....

App/Website/Company Name: ....

Website Address: ....

Username: ....

Password/Hint: ....

....

....

Code/PIN: ....

Phone: ....

Notes: ....

....

HEALTH

Calm, MyFitnessPal, Teladoc, etc.

App/Website/Company Name: ....

Website Address: ....

Username: ....

Password/Hint: ....

....

....

Code/PIN: ....

Phone: ....

Notes: ....

....

App/Website/Company Name: ....

Website Address: ....

Username: ....

Password/Hint: ....

....

....

Code/PIN: ....

Phone: ....

Notes: ....

....

App/Website/Company Name: ....

Website Address: ....

Username: ....

Password/Hint: ....

....

....

Code/PIN: ....

Phone: ....

Notes: ....

....

App/Website/Company Name: ....

Website Address: ....

Username: ....

Password/Hint: ....

....

....

Code/PIN: ....

Phone: ....

Notes: ....

....

INSURANCE

Progressive, State Farm, USAA, etc.

App/Website/
Company Name: ....

Website Address: ....

Username: ....

Password/Hint: ....

....

....

Code/PIN: ....

Phone: ....

Notes: ....

....

App/Website/Company Name: ....

Website Address: ....

Username: ....

Password/Hint: ....

....

....

Code/PIN: ....

Phone: ....

Notes: ....

....

App/Website/
Company Name: ....

Website Address: ....

Username: ....

Password/Hint: ....

....

....

Code/PIN: ....

Phone: ....

Notes: ....

....

App/Website/Company Name: ....

Website Address: ....

Username: ....

Password/Hint: ....

....

....

Code/PIN: ....

Phone: ....

Notes: ....

....

INSURANCE

Progressive, State Farm, USAA, etc.

App/Website/Company Name: ....

Website Address: ....

Username: ....

Password/Hint: ....

....

....

Code/PIN: ....

Phone: ....

Notes: ....

....

App/Website/Company Name: ....

Website Address: ....

Username: ....

Password/Hint: ....

....

....

Code/PIN: ....

Phone: ....

Notes: ....

....

APPS AND WEBSITES
FINANCE
HOME AND SECURITY
NETWORK
OTHER

App/Website/Company Name: ....

Website Address: ....

Username: ....

Password/Hint: ....

....

....

Code/PIN: ....

Phone: ....

Notes: ....

....

App/Website/Company Name: ....

Website Address: ....

Username: ....

Password/Hint: ....

....

....

Code/PIN: ....

Phone: ....

Notes: ....

....

LIVE EVENTS

Live Nation, Stubhub, Ticketmaster, etc.

App/Website/Company Name: ....

Website Address: ....

Username: ....

Password/Hint: ....

....

....

Code/PIN: ....

Phone: ....

Notes: ....

....

App/Website/Company Name: ....

Website Address: ....

Username: ....

Password/Hint: ....

....

....

Code/PIN: ....

Phone: ....

Notes: ....

....

App/Website/Company Name: ....

Website Address: ....

Username: ....

Password/Hint: ....

....

....

Code/PIN: ....

Phone: ....

Notes: ....

....

App/Website/Company Name: ....

Website Address: ....

Username: ....

Password/Hint: ....

....

....

Code/PIN: ....

Phone: ....

Notes: ....

....

LIVE EVENTS

Live Nation, Stubhub, Ticketmaster, etc.

App/Website/Company Name: ....

Website Address: ....

Username: ....

Password/Hint: ....

....

....

Code/PIN: ....

Phone: ....

Notes: ....

....

App/Website/Company Name: ....

Website Address: ....

Username: ....

Password/Hint: ....

....

....

Code/PIN: ....

Phone: ....

Notes: ....

....

APPS AND WEBSITES
FINANCE
HOME AND SECURITY
NETWORK
OTHER

App/Website/Company Name: ....

Website Address: ....

Username: ....

Password/Hint: ....

....

....

Code/PIN: ....

Phone: ....

Notes: ....

....

App/Website/Company Name: ....

Website Address: ....

Username: ....

Password/Hint: ....

....

....

Code/PIN: ....

Phone: ....

Notes: ....

....

APPS AND WEBSITES

FINANCE

HOME AND SECURITY

NETWORK

OTHER

MAPS/GPS

Google Maps, Life360, Waze, etc.

App/Website/Company Name: ....

Website Address: ....

Username: ....

Password/Hint: ....

....

....

Code/PIN: ....

Phone: ....

Notes: ....

....

App/Website/Company Name: ....

Website Address: ....

Username: ....

Password/Hint: ....

....

....

Code/PIN: ....

Phone: ....

Notes: ....

....

App/Website/Company Name: ....

Website Address: ....

Username: ....

Password/Hint: ....

....

....

Code/PIN: ....

Phone: ....

Notes: ....

....

App/Website/Company Name: ....

Website Address: ....

Username: ....

Password/Hint: ....

....

....

Code/PIN: ....

Phone: ....

Notes: ....

....

MEMBERSHIPS

AAA, AARP, Gym, etc.

App/Website/Company Name: ....

Website Address: ....

Username: ....

Password/Hint: ....

....

....

Code/PIN: ....

Phone: ....

Notes: ....

....

App/Website/Company Name: ....

Website Address: ....

Username: ....

Password/Hint: ....

....

....

Code/PIN: ....

Phone: ....

Notes: ....

....

APPS AND WEBSITES
FINANCE
HOME AND SECURITY
NETWORK
OTHER

App/Website/Company Name: ....

Website Address: ....

Username: ....

Password/Hint: ....

....

....

Code/PIN: ....

Phone: ....

Notes: ....

....

App/Website/Company Name: ....

Website Address: ....

Username: ....

Password/Hint: ....

....

....

Code/PIN: ....

Phone: ....

Notes: ....

....

MEMBERSHIPS

AAA, AARP, Gym, etc.

App/Website/Company Name: ....

Website Address: ....

Username: ....

Password/Hint: ....

....

....

Code/PIN: ....

Phone: ....

Notes: ....

....

App/Website/Company Name: ....

Website Address: ....

Username: ....

Password/Hint: ....

....

....

Code/PIN: ....

Phone: ....

Notes: ....

....

App/Website/Company Name: ....

Website Address: ....

Username: ....

Password/Hint: ....

....

....

Code/PIN: ....

Phone: ....

Notes: ....

....

App/Website/Company Name: ....

Website Address: ....

Username: ....

Password/Hint: ....

....

....

Code/PIN: ....

Phone: ....

Notes: ....

....

APPS AND WEBSITES

FINANCE

HOME AND SECURITY

NETWORK

OTHER

MOVIES/MUSIC

Deezer, Fandango, IMDb, etc.

App/Website/Company Name: ....

Website Address: ....

Username: ....

Password/Hint: ....

....

....

Code/PIN: ....

Phone: ....

Notes: ....

....

App/Website/Company Name: ....

Website Address: ....

Username: ....

Password/Hint: ....

....

....

Code/PIN: ....

Phone: ....

Notes: ....

....

App/Website/Company Name: ....

Website Address: ....

Username: ....

Password/Hint: ....

....

....

Code/PIN: ....

Phone: ....

Notes: ....

....

App/Website/Company Name: ....

Website Address: ....

Username: ....

Password/Hint: ....

....

....

Code/PIN: ....

Phone: ....

Notes: ....

....

APPS AND WEBSITES

FINANCE

HOME AND SECURITY

NETWORK

OTHER

MOVIES/MUSIC

Deezer, Fandango, IMDb, etc.

App/Website/Company Name: ....

Website Address: ....

Username: ....

Password/Hint: ....

....

....

Code/PIN: ....

Phone: ....

Notes: ....

....

App/Website/Company Name: ....

Website Address: ....

Username: ....

Password/Hint: ....

....

....

Code/PIN: ....

Phone: ....

Notes: ....

....

App/Website/Company Name: ....

Website Address: ....

Username: ....

Password/Hint: ....

....

....

Code/PIN: ....

Phone: ....

Notes: ....

....

App/Website/Company Name: ....

Website Address: ....

Username: ....

Password/Hint: ....

....

....

Code/PIN: ....

Phone: ....

Notes: ....

....

NEWS/WEATHER/SPORTS

Accuweather, The Athletic, WSJ, etc.

App/Website/Company Name: ....

Website Address: ....

Username: ....

Password/Hint: ....

....

....

Code/PIN: ....

Phone: ....

Notes: ....

....

App/Website/Company Name: ....

Website Address: ....

Username: ....

Password/Hint: ....

....

....

Code/PIN: ....

Phone: ....

Notes: ....

....

App/Website/Company Name: ....

Website Address: ....

Username: ....

Password/Hint: ....

....

....

Code/PIN: ....

Phone: ....

Notes: ....

....

App/Website/Company Name: ....

Website Address: ....

Username: ....

Password/Hint: ....

....

....

Code/PIN: ....

Phone: ....

Notes: ....

....

APPS AND WEBSITES

FINANCE

HOME AND SECURITY

NETWORK

OTHER

NEWS/WEATHER/SPORTS

Accuweather, The Athletic, WSJ, etc.

App/Website/Company Name: ....

Website Address: ....

Username: ....

Password/Hint: ....

....

....

Code/PIN: ....

Phone: ....

Notes: ....

....

App/Website/Company Name: ....

Website Address: ....

Username: ....

Password/Hint: ....

....

....

Code/PIN: ....

Phone: ....

Notes: ....

....

App/Website/Company Name: ....

Website Address: ....

Username: ....

Password/Hint: ....

....

....

Code/PIN: ....

Phone: ....

Notes: ....

....

App/Website/Company Name: ....

Website Address: ....

Username: ....

Password/Hint: ....

....

....

Code/PIN: ....

Phone: ....

Notes: ....

....

REAL ESTATE

Home Depot, Houzz, Zillow, etc.

App/Website/Company Name: ....

Website Address: ....

Username: ....

Password/Hint: ....

....

....

Code/PIN: ....

Phone: ....

Notes: ....

....

App/Website/Company Name: ....

Website Address: ....

Username: ....

Password/Hint: ....

....

....

Code/PIN: ....

Phone: ....

Notes: ....

....

App/Website/Company Name: ....

Website Address: ....

Username: ....

Password/Hint: ....

....

....

Code/PIN: ....

Phone: ....

Notes: ....

....

App/Website/Company Name: ....

Website Address: ....

Username: ....

Password/Hint: ....

....

....

Code/PIN: ....

Phone: ....

Notes: ....

....

REAL ESTATE

Home Depot, Houzz, Zillow, etc.

App/Website/Company Name: ....

Website Address: ....

Username: ....

Password/Hint: ....

....

....

Code/PIN: ....

Phone: ....

Notes: ....

....

App/Website/Company Name: ....

Website Address: ....

Username: ....

Password/Hint: ....

....

....

Code/PIN: ....

Phone: ....

Notes: ....

....

App/Website/Company Name: ....

Website Address: ....

Username: ....

Password/Hint: ....

....

....

Code/PIN: ....

Phone: ....

Notes: ....

....

App/Website/Company Name: ....

Website Address: ....

Username: ....

Password/Hint: ....

....

....

Code/PIN: ....

Phone: ....

Notes: ....

....

RIDESHARE

Lyft, Turo, Uber, etc.

App/Website/Company Name: ....

Website Address: ....

Username: ....

Password/Hint: ....

....

....

Code/PIN: ....

Phone: ....

Notes: ....

....

App/Website/Company Name: ....

Website Address: ....

Username: ....

Password/Hint: ....

....

....

Code/PIN: ....

Phone: ....

Notes: ....

....

App/Website/Company Name: ....

Website Address: ....

Username: ....

Password/Hint: ....

....

....

Code/PIN: ....

Phone: ....

Notes: ....

....

App/Website/Company Name: ....

Website Address: ....

Username: ....

Password/Hint: ....

....

....

Code/PIN: ....

Phone: ....

Notes: ....

....

SHOPPING

Amazon, Costco, Macy's, etc.

App/Website/Company Name: ....

Website Address: ....

Username: ....

Password/Hint: ....

....

....

Code/PIN: ....

Phone: ....

Notes: ....

....

App/Website/Company Name: ....

Website Address: ....

Username: ....

Password/Hint: ....

....

....

Code/PIN: ....

Phone: ....

Notes: ....

....

App/Website/Company Name: ....

Website Address: ....

Username: ....

Password/Hint: ....

....

....

Code/PIN: ....

Phone: ....

Notes: ....

....

App/Website/Company Name: ....

Website Address: ....

Username: ....

Password/Hint: ....

....

....

Code/PIN: ....

Phone: ....

Notes: ....

....

APPS AND WEBSITES

FINANCE

HOME AND SECURITY

NETWORK

OTHER

SHOPPING

Amazon, Costco, Macy's, etc.

App/Website/Company Name: ....

Website Address: ....

Username: ....

Password/Hint: ....

....

....

Code/PIN: ....

Phone: ....

Notes: ....

....

App/Website/Company Name: ....

Website Address: ....

Username: ....

Password/Hint: ....

....

....

Code/PIN: ....

Phone: ....

Notes: ....

....

App/Website/Company Name: ....

Website Address: ....

Username: ....

Password/Hint: ....

....

....

Code/PIN: ....

Phone: ....

Notes: ....

....

App/Website/Company Name: ....

Website Address: ....

Username: ....

Password/Hint: ....

....

....

Code/PIN: ....

Phone: ....

Notes: ....

....

APPS AND WEBSITES

FINANCE

HOME AND SECURITY

NETWORK

OTHER

SHOPPING

Amazon, Costco, Macy's, etc.

App/Website/Company Name: ....

Website Address: ....

Username: ....

Password/Hint: ....

....

....

Code/PIN: ....

Phone: ....

Notes: ....

....

App/Website/Company Name: ....

Website Address: ....

Username: ....

Password/Hint: ....

....

....

Code/PIN: ....

Phone: ....

Notes: ....

....

App/Website/Company Name: ....

Website Address: ....

Username: ....

Password/Hint: ....

....

....

Code/PIN: ....

Phone: ....

Notes: ....

....

App/Website/Company Name: ....

Website Address: ....

Username: ....

Password/Hint: ....

....

....

Code/PIN: ....

Phone: ....

Notes: ....

....

SOCIAL MEDIA

Facebook, LinkedIn, Twitter, etc.

App/Website/Company Name: ....

Website Address: ....

Username: ....

Password/Hint: ....

....

....

Code/PIN: ....

Phone: ....

Notes: ....

....

App/Website/Company Name: ....

Website Address: ....

Username: ....

Password/Hint: ....

....

....

Code/PIN: ....

Phone: ....

Notes: ....

....

App/Website/Company Name: ....

Website Address: ....

Username: ....

Password/Hint: ....

....

....

Code/PIN: ....

Phone: ....

Notes: ....

....

App/Website/Company Name: ....

Website Address: ....

Username: ....

Password/Hint: ....

....

....

Code/PIN: ....

Phone: ....

Notes: ....

....

SOCIAL MEDIA

Facebook, LinkedIn, Twitter, etc.

App/Website/Company Name: ....

Website Address: ....

Username: ....

Password/Hint: ....

....

....

Code/PIN: ....

Phone: ....

Notes: ....

....

App/Website/Company Name: ....

Website Address: ....

Username: ....

Password/Hint: ....

....

....

Code/PIN: ....

Phone: ....

Notes: ....

....

App/Website/Company Name: ....

Website Address: ....

Username: ....

Password/Hint: ....

....

....

Code/PIN: ....

Phone: ....

Notes: ....

....

App/Website/Company Name: ....

Website Address: ....

Username: ....

Password/Hint: ....

....

....

Code/PIN: ....

Phone: ....

Notes: ....

....

SOCIAL MEDIA

Facebook, LinkedIn, Twitter, etc.

App/Website/Company Name: ....

Website Address: ....

Username: ....

Password/Hint: ....

....

....

Code/PIN: ....

Phone: ....

Notes: ....

....

App/Website/Company Name: ....

Website Address: ....

Username: ....

Password/Hint: ....

....

....

Code/PIN: ....

Phone: ....

Notes: ....

....

App/Website/Company Name: ....

Website Address: ....

Username: ....

Password/Hint: ....

....

....

Code/PIN: ....

Phone: ....

Notes: ....

....

App/Website/Company Name: ....

Website Address: ....

Username: ....

Password/Hint: ....

....

....

Code/PIN: ....

Phone: ....

Notes: ....

....

APPS AND WEBSITES

FINANCE

HOME AND SECURITY

NETWORK

OTHER

STREAMING SERVICES

Hulu, Netflix, Spotify, etc.

App/Website/Company Name: ....

Website Address: ....

Username: ....

Password/Hint: ....

....

....

Code/PIN: ....

Phone: ....

Notes: ....

....

App/Website/Company Name: ....

Website Address: ....

Username: ....

Password/Hint: ....

....

....

Code/PIN: ....

Phone: ....

Notes: ....

....

App/Website/Company Name: ....
Website Address: ....
Username: ....
Password/Hint: ....
....
....
Code/PIN: ....
Phone: ....
Notes: ....
....

App/Website/Company Name: ....
Website Address: ....
Username: ....
Password/Hint: ....
....
....
Code/PIN: ....
Phone: ....
Notes: ....
....

STREAMING SERVICES

Hulu, Netflix, Spotify, etc.

App/Website/Company Name: ....

Website Address: ....

Username: ....

Password/Hint: ....

....

....

Code/PIN: ....

Phone: ....

Notes: ....

....

App/Website/Company Name: ....

Website Address: ....

Username: ....

Password/Hint: ....

....

....

Code/PIN: ....

Phone: ....

Notes: ....

....

App/Website/Company Name: ....
Website Address: ....
Username: ....
Password/Hint: ....
....
....
Code/PIN: ....
Phone: ....
Notes: ....
....

App/Website/Company Name: ....
Website Address: ....
Username: ....
Password/Hint: ....
....
....
Code/PIN: ....
Phone: ....
Notes: ....
....

STREAMING SERVICES

Hulu, Netflix, Spotify, etc.

App/Website/Company Name: ....

Website Address: ....

Username: ....

Password/Hint: ....

....

....

Code/PIN: ....

Phone: ....

Notes: ....

....

App/Website/Company Name: ....

Website Address: ....

Username: ....

Password/Hint: ....

....

....

Code/PIN: ....

Phone: ....

Notes: ....

....

App/Website/Company Name: ....

Website Address: ....

Username: ....

Password/Hint: ....

....

....

Code/PIN: ....

Phone: ....

Notes: ....

....

App/Website/Company Name: ....

Website Address: ....

Username: ....

Password/Hint: ....

....

....

Code/PIN: ....

Phone: ....

Notes: ....

....

APPS AND WEBSITES

FINANCE

HOME AND SECURITY

NETWORK

OTHER

TRAVEL

American Airlines, Expedia, Marriott, etc.

App/Website/Company Name: ....

Website Address: ....

Username: ....

Password/Hint: ....

....

....

Code/PIN: ....

Phone: ....

Notes: ....

....

App/Website/Company Name: ....

Website Address: ....

Username: ....

Password/Hint: ....

....

....

Code/PIN: ....

Phone: ....

Notes: ....

....

App/Website/Company Name: ....

Website Address: ....

Username: ....

Password/Hint: ....

....

....

Code/PIN: ....

Phone: ....

Notes: ....

....

App/Website/Company Name: ....

Website Address: ....

Username: ....

Password/Hint: ....

....

....

Code/PIN: ....

Phone: ....

Notes: ....

....

TRAVEL

American Airlines, Expedia, Marriott, etc.

App/Website/Company Name: ....

Website Address: ....

Username: ....

Password/Hint: ....

....

....

Code/PIN: ....

Phone: ....

Notes: ....

....

App/Website/Company Name: ....

Website Address: ....

Username: ....

Password/Hint: ....

....

....

Code/PIN: ....

Phone: ....

Notes: ....

....

App/Website/Company Name: ....

Website Address: ....

Username: ....

Password/Hint: ....

....

....

Code/PIN: ....

Phone: ....

Notes: ....

....

App/Website/Company Name: ....

Website Address: ....

Username: ....

Password/Hint: ....

....

....

Code/PIN: ....

Phone: ....

Notes: ....

....

TRAVEL

American Airlines, Expedia, Marriott, etc.

App/Website/Company Name: ....

Website Address: ....

Username: ....

Password/Hint: ....

....

....

Code/PIN: ....

Phone: ....

Notes: ....

....

App/Website/Company Name: ....

Website Address: ....

Username: ....

Password/Hint: ....

....

....

Code/PIN: ....

Phone: ....

Notes: ....

....

App/Website/Company Name: ....

Website Address: ....

Username: ....

Password/Hint: ....

....

....

Code/PIN: ....

Phone: ....

Notes: ....

....

App/Website/Company Name: ....

Website Address: ....

Username: ....

Password/Hint: ....

....

....

Code/PIN: ....

Phone: ....

Notes: ....

....

APPS AND WEBSITES (OTHER)

App/Website/Company Name: ....

Website Address: ....

Username: ....

Password/Hint: ....

....

....

Code/PIN: ....

Phone: ....

Notes: ....

....

App/Website/Company Name: ....

Website Address: ....

Username: ....

Password/Hint: ....

....

....

Code/PIN: ....

Phone: ....

Notes: ....

....

App/Website/Company Name: ....

Website Address: ....

Username: ....

Password/Hint: ....

....

....

Code/PIN: ....

Phone: ....

Notes: ....

....

App/Website/Company Name: ....

Website Address: ....

Username: ....

Password/Hint: ....

....

....

Code/PIN: ....

Phone: ....

Notes: ....

....

APPS AND WEBSITES

FINANCE

HOME AND SECURITY

NETWORK

OTHER

APPS AND WEBSITES (OTHER)

App/Website/Company Name: ....

Website Address: ....

Username: ....

Password/Hint: ....

....

....

Code/PIN: ....

Phone: ....

Notes: ....

....

App/Website/Company Name: ....

Website Address: ....

Username: ....

Password/Hint: ....

....

....

Code/PIN: ....

Phone: ....

Notes: ....

....

App/Website/Company Name: ....

Website Address: ....

Username: ....

Password/Hint: ....

....

....

Code/PIN: ....

Phone: ....

Notes: ....

....

App/Website/Company Name: ....

Website Address: ....

Username: ....

Password/Hint: ....

....

....

Code/PIN: ....

Phone: ....

Notes: ....

....

APPS AND WEBSITES

FINANCE

HOME AND SECURITY

NETWORK

OTHER

APPS AND WEBSITES (OTHER)

App/Website/Company Name: ....

Website Address: ....

Username: ....

Password/Hint: ....

....

....

Code/PIN: ....

Phone: ....

Notes: ....

....

App/Website/Company Name: ....

Website Address: ....

Username: ....

Password/Hint: ....

....

....

Code/PIN: ....

Phone: ....

Notes: ....

....

App/Website/Company Name: ....

Website Address: ....

Username: ....

Password/Hint: ....

....

....

Code/PIN: ....

Phone: ....

Notes: ....

....

App/Website/Company Name: ....

Website Address: ....

Username: ....

Password/Hint: ....

....

....

Code/PIN: ....

Phone: ....

Notes: ....

....

APPS AND WEBSITES

FINANCE

HOME AND SECURITY

NETWORK

OTHER

BANKS, BILL PAY, ETC.

App/Website/Company Name:

Website Address:

Username:

Password/Hint:

Code/PIN:

Phone:

Notes:

App/Website/Company Name:

Website Address:

Username:

Password/Hint:

Code/PIN:

Phone:

Notes:

App/Website/Company Name:
Website Address:
Username:
Password/Hint:

Code/PIN:
Phone:
Notes:

App/Website/Company Name:
Website Address:
Username:
Password/Hint:

Code/PIN:
Phone:
Notes:

BANKS, BILL PAY, ETC.

App/Website/Company Name:

Website Address:

Username:

Password/Hint:

Code/PIN:

Phone:

Notes:

App/Website/Company Name:

Website Address:

Username:

Password/Hint:

Code/PIN:

Phone:

Notes:

App/Website/Company Name: ....

Website Address: ....

Username: ....

Password/Hint: ....

....

....

Code/PIN: ....

Phone: ....

Notes: ....

....

App/Website/Company Name: ....

Website Address: ....

Username: ....

Password/Hint: ....

....

....

Code/PIN: ....

Phone: ....

Notes: ....

....

BROKERAGE ACCOUNTS

App/Website/Company Name: ....

Website Address: ....

Username: ....

Password/Hint: ....

....

....

Code/PIN: ....

Phone: ....

Notes: ....

....

App/Website/Company Name: ....

Website Address: ....

Username: ....

Password/Hint: ....

....

....

Code/PIN: ....

Phone: ....

Notes: ....

....

App/Website/Company Name: ....

Website Address: ....

Username: ....

Password/Hint: ....

....

....

Code/PIN: ....

Phone: ....

Notes: ....

....

App/Website/Company Name: ....

Website Address: ....

Username: ....

Password/Hint: ....

....

....

Code/PIN: ....

Phone: ....

Notes: ....

....

CREDIT/ATM CARDS

App/Website/Company Name:

Website Address:

Username:

Password/Hint:

Code/PIN:

Phone:

Notes:

App/Website/Company Name:

Website Address:

Username:

Password/Hint:

Code/PIN:

Phone:

Notes:

App/Website/Company Name: ....

Website Address: ....

Username: ....

Password/Hint: ....

....

....

Code/PIN: ....

Phone: ....

Notes: ....

....

App/Website/Company Name: ....

Website Address: ....

Username: ....

Password/Hint: ....

....

....

Code/PIN: ....

Phone: ....

Notes: ....

....

CREDIT/ATM CARDS

App/Website/Company Name:

Website Address:

Username:

Password/Hint:

Code/PIN:

Phone:

Notes:

App/Website/Company Name:

Website Address:

Username:

Password/Hint:

Code/PIN:

Phone:

Notes:

App/Website/Company Name:

Website Address:

Username:

Password/Hint:

Code/PIN:

Phone:

Notes:

App/Website/Company Name:

Website Address:

Username:

Password/Hint:

Code/PIN:

Phone:

Notes:

CREDIT/ATM CARDS

App/Website/Company Name: ....

Website Address: ....

Username: ....

Password/Hint: ....

....

....

Code/PIN: ....

Phone: ....

Notes: ....

....

App/Website/Company Name: ....

Website Address: ....

Username: ....

Password/Hint: ....

....

....

Code/PIN: ....

Phone: ....

Notes: ....

....

App/Website/Company Name: ....

Website Address: ....

Username: ....

Password/Hint: ....

....

....

Code/PIN: ....

Phone: ....

Notes: ....

....

App/Website/Company Name: ....

Website Address: ....

Username: ....

Password/Hint: ....

....

....

Code/PIN: ....

Phone: ....

Notes: ....

....

FINANCIAL SOFTWARE

App/Website/Company Name:

Website Address:

Username:

Password/Hint:

Code/PIN:

Phone:

Notes:

App/Website/Company Name:

Website Address:

Username:

Password/Hint:

Code/PIN:

Phone:

Notes:

App/Website/Company Name: ....

Website Address: ....

Username: ....

Password/Hint: ....

....

....

Code/PIN: ....

Phone: ....

Notes: ....

....

App/Website/Company Name: ....

Website Address: ....

Username: ....

Password/Hint: ....

....

....

Code/PIN: ....

Phone: ....

Notes: ....

....

MORTGAGE, LOANS, RENT, ETC.

App/Website/Company Name:

Website Address:

Username:

Password/Hint:

Code/PIN:

Phone:

Notes:

App/Website/Company Name:

Website Address:

Username:

Password/Hint:

Code/PIN:

Phone:

Notes:

App/Website/Company Name:

Website Address:

Username:

Password/Hint:

Code/PIN:

Phone:

Notes:

App/Website/Company Name:

Website Address:

Username:

Password/Hint:

Code/PIN:

Phone:

Notes:

PEER-TO-PEER

App/Website/Company Name:

Website Address:

Username:

Password/Hint:

Code/PIN:

Phone:

Notes:

App/Website/Company Name:

Website Address:

Username:

Password/Hint:

Code/PIN:

Phone:

Notes:

APPS AND WEBSITES
FINANCE
HOME AND SECURITY
NETWORK
OTHER

App/Website/Company Name:

Website Address:

Username:

Password/Hint:

Code/PIN:

Phone:

Notes:

App/Website/Company Name:

Website Address:

Username:

Password/Hint:

Code/PIN:

Phone:

Notes:

RETIREMENT ACCOUNTS

App/Website/Company Name: ....

Website Address: ....

Username: ....

Password/Hint: ....

....

....

Code/PIN: ....

Phone: ....

Notes: ....

....

App/Website/Company Name: ....

Website Address: ....

Username: ....

Password/Hint: ....

....

....

Code/PIN: ....

Phone: ....

Notes: ....

....

App/Website/Company Name:
Website Address:
Username:
Password/Hint:

Code/PIN:
Phone:
Notes:

App/Website/Company Name:
Website Address:
Username:
Password/Hint:

Code/PIN:
Phone:
Notes:

APPS AND WEBSITES
FINANCE
HOME AND SECURITY
NETWORK
OTHER

FINANCE (OTHER)

App/Website/Company Name: ....

Website Address: ....

Username: ....

Password/Hint: ....

....

....

Code/PIN: ....

Phone: ....

Notes: ....

....

App/Website/Company Name: ....

Website Address: ....

Username: ....

Password/Hint: ....

....

....

Code/PIN: ....

Phone: ....

Notes: ....

....

App/Website/Company Name:

Website Address:

Username:

Password/Hint:

Code/PIN:

Phone:

Notes:

App/Website/Company Name:

Website Address:

Username:

Password/Hint:

Code/PIN:

Phone:

Notes:

APPLIANCES

iRobot, Maytag, Whirlpool, etc.

App/Website/Company Name: ....

Website Address: ....

Username: ....

Password/Hint: ....

....

....

Code/PIN: ....

Phone: ....

Notes: ....

....

App/Website/Company Name: ....

Website Address: ....

Username: ....

Password/Hint: ....

....

....

Code/PIN: ....

Phone: ....

Notes: ....

....

App/Website/Company Name: ....

Website Address: ....

Username: ....

Password/Hint: ....

....

....

Code/PIN: ....

Phone: ....

Notes: ....

....

App/Website/Company Name: ....

Website Address: ....

Username: ....

Password/Hint: ....

....

....

Code/PIN: ....

Phone: ....

Notes: ....

....

CAR ALARM

App/Website/Company Name:

Website Address:

Username:

Password/Hint:

Code/PIN:

Phone:

Notes:

GARAGE DOOR

App/Website/Company Name:

Website Address:

Username:

Password/Hint:

Code/PIN:

Phone:

Notes:

HOME SAFE

App/Website/Company Name:

Website Address:

Username:

Password/Hint:

Code/PIN:

Phone:

Notes:

HOME SECURITY SYSTEM

App/Website/Company Name:

Website Address:

Username:

Password/Hint:

Code/PIN:

Phone:

Notes:

GATE

App/Website/Company Name: ....

Website Address: ....

Username: ....

Password/Hint: ....

....

....

Code/PIN: ....

Phone: ....

Notes: ....

....

GUN SAFE

App/Website/Company Name: ....

Website Address: ....

Username: ....

Password/Hint: ....

....

....

Code/PIN: ....

Phone: ....

Notes: ....

MAILBOX

App/Website/Company Name:

Website Address:

Username:

Password/Hint:

Code/PIN:

Phone:

Notes:

SAFETY DEPOSIT BOX

App/Website/Company Name:

Website Address:

Username:

Password/Hint:

Code/PIN:

Phone:

Notes:

SMART LOCKS, DOORBELLS, ETC.

App/Website/Company Name:

Website Address:

Username:

Password/Hint:

Code/PIN:

Phone:

Notes:

App/Website/Company Name:

Website Address:

Username:

Password/Hint:

Code/PIN:

Phone:

Notes:

THERMOSTAT

Carrier, Honeywell, Nest, etc.

App/Website/Company Name: ....

Website Address: ....

Username: ....

Password/Hint: ....

....

....

Code/PIN: ....

Phone: ....

Notes: ....

....

App/Website/Company Name: ....

Website Address: ....

Username: ....

Password/Hint: ....

....

....

Code/PIN: ....

Phone: ....

Notes: ....

....

HOME AND SECURITY (OTHER)

App/Website/Company Name: ....
Website Address: ....
Username: ....
Password/Hint: ....
....
....
Code/PIN: ....
Phone: ....
Notes: ....
....

App/Website/Company Name: ....
Website Address: ....
Username: ....
Password/Hint: ....
....
....
Code/PIN: ....
Phone: ....
Notes: ....
....

App/Website/Company Name:

Website Address:

Username:

Password/Hint:

Code/PIN:

Phone:

Notes:

App/Website/Company Name:

Website Address:

Username:

Password/Hint:

Code/PIN:

Phone:

Notes:

HOME AND SECURITY (OTHER)

App/Website/Company Name:

Website Address:

Username:

Password/Hint:

Code/PIN:

Phone:

Notes:

App/Website/Company Name:

Website Address:

Username:

Password/Hint:

Code/PIN:

Phone:

Notes:

App/Website/Company Name: ....

Website Address: ....

Username: ....

Password/Hint: ....

....

....

Code/PIN: ....

Phone: ....

Notes: ....

....

App/Website/Company Name: ....

Website Address: ....

Username: ....

Password/Hint: ....

....

....

Code/PIN: ....

Phone: ....

Notes: ....

....

WIFI HOME NETWORK

Network Name (SSID): ....

Network Password/Key: ....

Printer: ....

MODEM

Username: ....

Password: ....

ROUTER/WIRELESS ACCESS

WAN/LAN Settings: ....

Notes: ....

....

....

....

SOFTWARE LICENSE NUMBERS

Software Name: ....

License Number: ....

Purchase Date: ....

Software Name: ....

License Number: ....

Purchase Date: ....

Software Name: ....

License Number: ....

Purchase Date: ....

Software Name: ....

License Number: ....

Purchase Date: ....

Software Name: ....

License Number: ....

Purchase Date: ....

Software Name: ....

License Number: ....

Purchase Date: ....

APPS AND WEBSITES

FINANCE

HOME AND SECURITY

NETWORK

OTHER

EMAIL ACCOUNT SETTINGS

Email Address: ....

Mail Server: ....

Incoming Server: ....

....

Outgoing Server: ....

....

Username: ....

Password: ....

EMAIL ACCOUNT SETTINGS

Email Address: ....

Mail Server: ....

Incoming Server: ....

....

Outgoing Server: ....

....

Username: ....

Password: ....

EMAIL ACCOUNT SETTINGS

Email Address: ....

Mail Server: ....

Incoming Server: ....

....

Outgoing Server: ....

....

Username: ....

Password: ....

EMAIL ACCOUNT SETTINGS

Email Address: ....

Mail Server: ....

Incoming Server: ....

....

Outgoing Server: ....

....

Username: ....

Password: ....

NETWORK (OTHER)

App/Website/Company Name:

Website Address:

Username:

Password/Hint:

Code/PIN:

Phone:

Notes:

App/Website/Company Name:

Website Address:

Username:

Password/Hint:

Code/PIN:

Phone:

Notes:

App/Website/Company Name:

Website Address:

Username:

Password/Hint:

Code/PIN:

Phone:

Notes:

App/Website/Company Name:

Website Address:

Username:

Password/Hint:

Code/PIN:

Phone:

Notes:

NETWORK (OTHER)

App/Website/Company Name: ....

Website Address: ....

Username: ....

Password/Hint: ....

....

....

Code/PIN: ....

Phone: ....

Notes: ....

....

App/Website/Company Name: ....

Website Address: ....

Username: ....

Password/Hint: ....

....

....

Code/PIN: ....

Phone: ....

Notes: ....

....

App/Website/Company Name:
Website Address:
Username:
Password/Hint:

Code/PIN:
Phone:
Notes:

App/Website/Company Name:
Website Address:
Username:
Password/Hint:

Code/PIN:
Phone:
Notes:

OTHER

App/Website/Company Name: ....

Website Address: ....

Username: ....

Password/Hint: ....

....

....

Code/PIN: ....

Phone: ....

Notes: ....

....

App/Website/Company Name: ....

Website Address: ....

Username: ....

Password/Hint: ....

....

....

Code/PIN: ....

Phone: ....

Notes: ....

....

App/Website/Company Name: ....

Website Address: ....

Username: ....

Password/Hint: ....

....

....

Code/PIN: ....

Phone: ....

Notes: ....

....

App/Website/Company Name: ....

Website Address: ....

Username: ....

Password/Hint: ....

....

....

Code/PIN: ....

Phone: ....

Notes: ....

....

OTHER

App/Website/Company Name: ....

Website Address: ....

Username: ....

Password/Hint: ....

....

....

Code/PIN: ....

Phone: ....

Notes: ....

....

App/Website/Company Name: ....

Website Address: ....

Username: ....

Password/Hint: ....

....

....

Code/PIN: ....

Phone: ....

Notes: ....

....

App/Website/Company Name:

Website Address:

Username:

Password/Hint:

Code/PIN:

Phone:

Notes:

App/Website/Company Name:

Website Address:

Username:

Password/Hint:

Code/PIN:

Phone:

Notes:

OTHER

App/Website/Company Name:

Website Address:

Username:

Password/Hint:

Code/PIN:

Phone:

Notes:

App/Website/Company Name:

Website Address:

Username:

Password/Hint:

Code/PIN:

Phone:

Notes:

App/Website/Company Name:

Website Address:

Username:

Password/Hint:

Code/PIN:

Phone:

Notes:

App/Website/Company Name:

Website Address:

Username:

Password/Hint:

Code/PIN:

Phone:

Notes:

OTHER

App/Website/Company Name:

Website Address:

Username:

Password/Hint:

Code/PIN:

Phone:

Notes:

App/Website/Company Name:

Website Address:

Username:

Password/Hint:

Code/PIN:

Phone:

Notes:

App/Website/Company Name:

Website Address:

Username:

Password/Hint:

Code/PIN:

Phone:

Notes:

App/Website/Company Name:

Website Address:

Username:

Password/Hint:

Code/PIN:

Phone:

Notes:

OTHER

App/Website/Company Name:

Website Address:

Username:

Password/Hint:

Code/PIN:

Phone:

Notes:

App/Website/Company Name:

Website Address:

Username:

Password/Hint:

Code/PIN:

Phone:

Notes:

App/Website/Company Name:

Website Address:

Username:

Password/Hint:

Code/PIN:

Phone:

Notes:

App/Website/Company Name:

Website Address:

Username:

Password/Hint:

Code/PIN:

Phone:

Notes:

OTHER

App/Website/Company Name: ....

Website Address: ....

Username: ....

Password/Hint: ....

....

....

Code/PIN: ....

Phone: ....

Notes: ....

....

App/Website/Company Name: ....

Website Address: ....

Username: ....

Password/Hint: ....

....

....

Code/PIN: ....

Phone: ....

Notes: ....

....

App/Website/Company Name:

Website Address:

Username:

Password/Hint:

Code/PIN:

Phone:

Notes:

App/Website/Company Name:

Website Address:

Username:

Password/Hint:

Code/PIN:

Phone:

Notes:

APPS AND WEBSITES
FINANCE
HOME AND SECURITY
NETWORK
OTHER

OTHER

App/Website/Company Name: ....

Website Address: ....

Username: ....

Password/Hint: ....

....

....

Code/PIN: ....

Phone: ....

Notes: ....

....

App/Website/Company Name: ....

Website Address: ....

Username: ....

Password/Hint: ....

....

....

Code/PIN: ....

Phone: ....

Notes: ....

....

App/Website/Company Name:

Website Address:

Username:

Password/Hint:

Code/PIN:

Phone:

Notes:

App/Website/Company Name:

Website Address:

Username:

Password/Hint:

Code/PIN:

Phone:

Notes:

Made in United States
Troutdale, OR
11/03/2026

56845234R00086